MW01245095

# KANSAS CITY CHIEFS

## BY BRIAN HOWELL

Published by The Child's World®
1980 Lookout Drive • Mankato, MN 56003-1705
800-599-READ • www.childsworld.com

Acknowledgments
The Child's World®: Mary Berendes, Publishing Director
Red Line Editorial: Editorial direction
The Design Lab: Design
Amnet: Production

Design Element: Dean Bertoncelj/Shutterstock Images
Photographs ©: Greg Trott/AP Images, cover; Rick
Scuteri/AP Images, 5; NFL Photos/AP Images, 7, 23; AP
Images, 9; Hector Acevedo/ZumaPress/Icon Sportswire,
11; Shutterstock, 13; Reed Hoffmann/AP Images, 14–15, 25;
G. Newman Lowrance/AP Images, 17; Ed Zurga/AP
Images, 19; Colin E. Braley/AP Images, 21; Lynne Sladky/
AP Images, 27; Scott D. Weaver/Icon Sportswire, 29

ISBN 9781634070003
LCCN 2014959707

Printed in the United States of America
Mankato, MN
May, 2016
PA02315

## ABOUT THE AUTHOR

Brian Howell is a freelance writer based in Denver, Colorado. He has been a sports journalist for nearly 20 years and has written dozens of books about sports and two about American history. A native of Colorado, he lives with his wife and four children in his home state.

# TABLE OF CONTENTS

# GO, CHIEFS!

**T**he Kansas City Chiefs have great fans. The team has given them a lot to cheer about. The Chiefs have had several **Hall of Fame** players. They had some good early years. Kansas City has won one **Super Bowl** and played in another. But they have not been back to the big game since 1970. Fans cannot wait to celebrate another title. Let's meet the Chiefs.

*Tight end Travis Kelce runs with the ball in a game against the Arizona Cardinals on December 7, 2014.*

# WHO ARE THE CHIEFS?

**T**he Kansas City Chiefs play in the National Football **League** (NFL). They are one of the 32 teams in the NFL. The NFL includes the American Football Conference (AFC) and the National Football Conference (NFC). The winner of the AFC plays the winner of the NFC in the Super Bowl. The Chiefs play in the West Division of the AFC. Kansas City won the Super Bowl after the 1969 season. The team also won an American Football League (AFL) Championship as the Dallas Texans in 1962.

*The Chiefs huddle up during their 23-7 win over the Minnesota Vikings in the Super Bowl on January 11, 1970.*

# WHERE THEY CAME FROM

**A** new professional football league was formed in 1960. It was called the AFL. One of its first teams was the Dallas Texans. Texans owner Lamar Hunt wanted to move the team after three seasons. Dallas already had the NFL's Cowboys. The city could not support two teams. So the Texans moved to Kansas City in 1963. The team kept its red, white, and yellow colors. But Hunt changed its nickname to the Chiefs.

*Tommy Brooker (81) kicked the winning field goal in overtime when the Dallas Texans beat the Houston Oilers 20-17 in the AFL Championship Game on December 23, 1962.*

# WHO THEY PLAY

The Kansas City Chiefs play 16 games each season. With so few games, each one is important. Every year, the Chiefs play two games against each of the other three teams in their division. Those teams are the Denver Broncos, Oakland Raiders, and San Diego Chargers. The Chiefs also play six other teams from the AFC and four from the NFC. The Chiefs have been **rivals** with the other AFC West teams for more than 50 years. The Raiders have been the Chiefs' biggest rival. They always play each other hard.

*The Chiefs have played their AFC West rivals, including the Denver Broncos, every year since 1960.*

# WHERE THEY PLAY

**T**he Dallas Texans played in the Cotton Bowl from 1960 to 1962. Then the team moved to Kansas City. The Chiefs played in Municipal Stadium from 1963 to 1971. Now they call Arrowhead Stadium home. The Chiefs have been there since 1972. Arrowhead holds nearly 77,000 fans. They go crazy during games. The noise bothers other teams on offense. That makes it hard to beat Kansas City at home.

*The Chiefs lost the first regular season football game in Arrowhead Stadium 20-10 to the New Orleans Saints on September 17, 1972.*

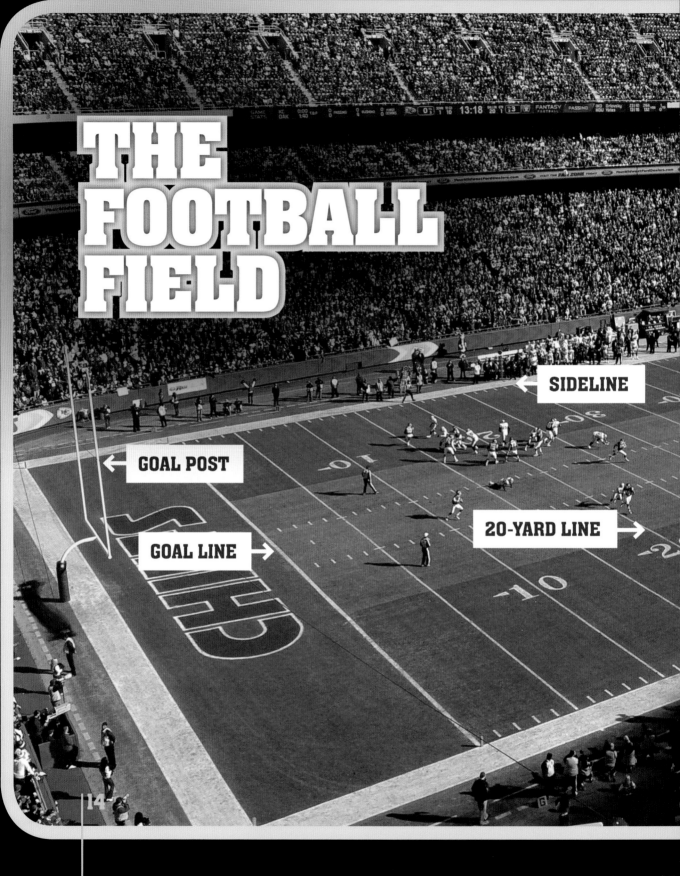

# THE FOOTBALL FIELD

SIDELINE

GOAL POST

GOAL LINE

20-YARD LINE

14

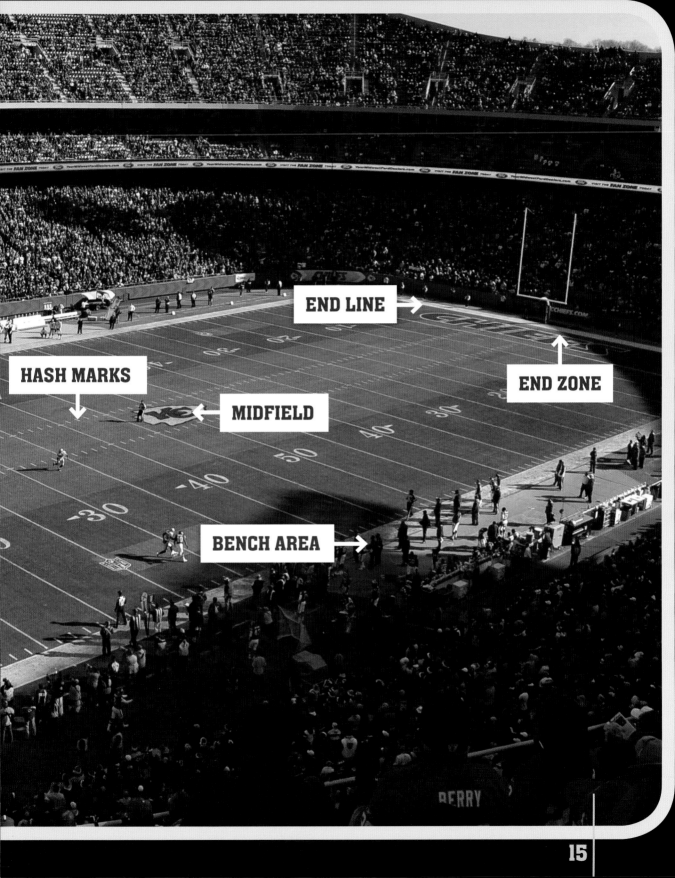

END LINE

END ZONE

HASH MARKS

MIDFIELD

BENCH AREA

# BIG DAYS

**T**he Chiefs have had some great moments in their history. Here are three of the greatest:

**1962**—The Dallas Texans' last season was special. The team won the West Division title. Then the Texans beat the Houston Oilers 20-17 in double **overtime** to win the AFL Championship.

**1969**—The 1969 Chiefs won the Super Bowl on January 11, 1970. Kansas City beat the Minnesota Vikings 23-7. The Chiefs defense forced five turnovers.

**1993**—Kansas City traded for Joe Montana on April 20. He was one of the best quarterbacks of all time. He had

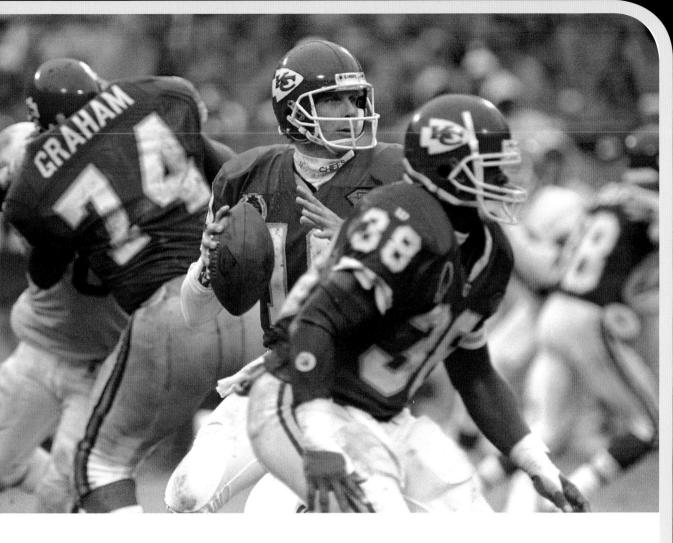

*Chiefs fans got to cheer on legendary quarterback Joe Montana for two seasons.*

led the San Francisco 49ers to four Super Bowl wins. Montana took Kansas City to the playoffs twice. He then retired before the 1995 season.

# TOUGH DAYS

**F**ootball is a hard game. Even the best teams have rough games and seasons. Here are some of the toughest times in Chiefs history:

**1971**—Kansas City met the Miami Dolphins in the playoffs. It was Christmas Day. The Chiefs lost 27-24 in double overtime. The game lasted 82 minutes and 40 seconds. It is still the longest game in NFL history.

**1995**—The 1995 Chiefs had high hopes for the playoffs. They met the Indianapolis Colts in the second round on January 7, 1996. Kansas City was expected to win. But kicker Lin Elliott missed three **field goals**. The Chiefs lost 10-7.

*Kansas City kicker Lin Elliott missed three field goals during the Chiefs' 10-7 playoff loss to the Indianapolis Colts on January 7, 1996.*

**2012**—This was one of the worst seasons in team history. The Chiefs scored the fewest points in the NFL. They ended the season 2-14. Coach Romeo Crennel was fired.

# MEET THE FANS

**C**hiefs fans are some of the loudest in sports. They prove that by packing Arrowhead Stadium. Fans were really excited on September 29, 2014. The Chiefs played the New England Patriots on *Monday Night Football*. That night, fans broke the Guinness World Record for the loudest stadium crowd. The noise reached 142.2 decibels. That is louder than a jet airplane flying 100 feet overhead.

*Kansas City fans got extra loud on September 29, 2014, against the New England Patriots.*

# HEROES THEN

**H**ank Stram coached the team from 1960 to 1974. He led it to an AFL Championship win and a Super Bowl title. Quarterback Len Dawson was the **Most Valuable Player** of the Super Bowl win. The defense had five Hall of Fame players, led by linebacker Willie Lanier. Tony Gonzalez is one of the best tight ends ever. He played with the Chiefs from 1997 to 2008. He made the **Pro Bowl** in each of his final ten years in Kansas City. Running back Priest Holmes was a star. He led the NFL in rushing touchdowns in 2002 and 2003. Linebacker Derrick Thomas was an awesome pass rusher. He made the Pro Bowl every year from 1989 to 1997.

*Quarterback Len Dawson (16) was inducted into the Pro Football Hall of Fame in 1987.*

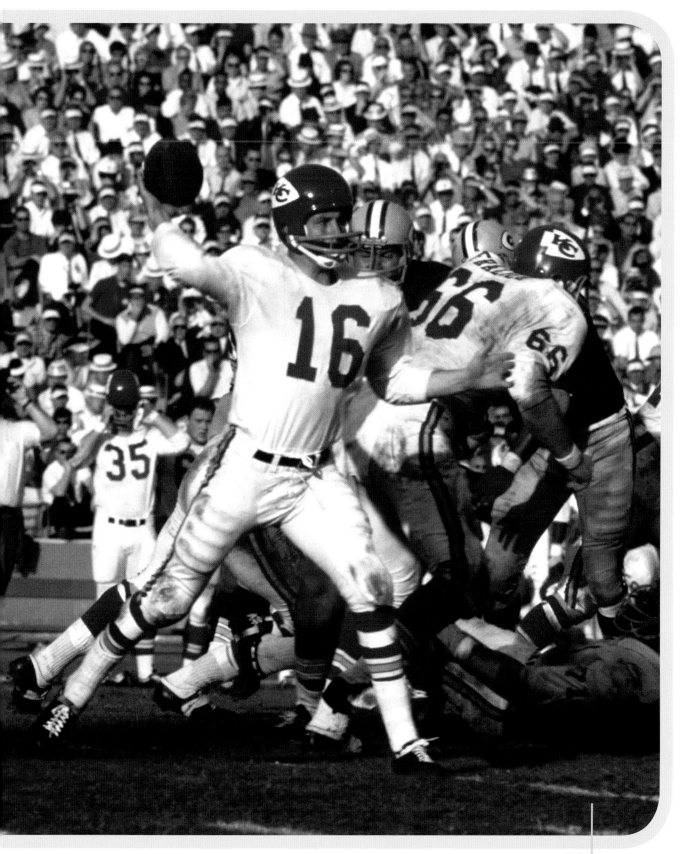

# HEROES NOW

**R**unning back Jamaal Charles is an exciting playmaker. He rushed for more than 1,100 yards in four of his first six seasons in the NFL. Charles can score from anywhere. Quarterback Alex Smith joined Kansas City in 2013. He helped the Chiefs return to the playoffs. Wide receiver Jeremy Maclin arrived in 2015. He is a great player when healthy. Coach Andy Reid has built a strong defense. It had six Pro Bowl players in 2013. Two of them were defensive end Tamba Hali and linebacker Justin Houston. They make life hard on opposing quarterbacks.

*Linebacker Justin Houston (50) had at least ten sacks each year from 2012 to 2014.*

# GEARING UP

**N**FL players wear team uniforms. They wear helmets and pads to keep them safe. Cleats help them make quick moves and run fast. Some players wear extra gear for protection.

## THE FOOTBALL

NFL footballs are made of leather. Under the leather is a lining that fills with air to give the ball its shape. The leather has bumps or "pebbles." These help players grip the ball. Laces help players control their throws. Footballs are also called "pigskins" because some of the first balls were made from pig bladders. Today they are made of leather from cows.

*Quarterback Alex Smith prepares to throw during a game against the Miami Dolphins on September 21, 2014.*

HELMET →

CHIN STRAP →

← SHOULDER PADS

THIGH PADS

FOOTBALL

# SPORTS STATS

**H**ere are some of the all-time career records for the Kansas City Chiefs. All the stats are through the 2014 season:

## PASSING YARDS

Len Dawson 28,507

Trent Green 21,459

## RUSHING YARDS

Jamaal Charles 6,856

Priest Holmes 6,070

## TOTAL TOUCHDOWNS

Priest Holmes 83

Tony Gonzalez 76

## INTERCEPTIONS

Emmitt Thomas 58

Johnny Robinson 57

## SACKS

Derrick Thomas 126.5

Neil Smith 85.5

## POINTS

Nick Lowery 1,466

Jan Stenerud 1,231

*Tight end Tony Gonzalez is one of the best players in Chiefs history.*

## RECEPTIONS

Tony Gonzalez 916

Dwayne Bowe 532

# GLOSSARY

**field goals** a method of scoring worth three points in which a player kicks the ball between the goal posts

**Hall of Fame** a museum in Canton, Ohio, that honors the best players

**league** an organization of sports teams that compete against each other

**Most Valuable Player** a yearly award given to the top player in the NFL

**overtime** extra time that is played when teams are tied at the end of four quarters

**Pro Bowl** the NFL's All-Star game where the best players in the league compete

**rivals** teams whose games bring out the greatest emotion between the players and the fans on both sides

**Super Bowl** the championship game of the NFL, played between the winners of the AFC and the NFC

# FIND OUT MORE

## IN THE LIBRARY

Frisch, Nate. *The Story of the Kansas City Chiefs.*
Mankato, MN: Creative Education, 2014.

Fulks, Matt. *100 Things Chiefs Fans Should Know & Do
Before They Die.* Chicago: Triumph Books, 2014.

Stallard, Mark. *Kansas City Chiefs Encyclopedia.*
New York: Sports Publishing, 2013.

## ON THE WEB

Visit our Web site for links about the Kansas City Chiefs:
**childsworld.com/links**

*Note to Parents, Teachers, and Librarians: We routinely verify our Web links to make
sure they are safe and active sites. So encourage your readers to check them out!*

# INDEX